In Some
Foreign Field

Grape and Canister

*The Story of the Field Artillery
of the Army of the Potomac
1861–1865*

In Some Foreign Field

*The Story
of Four British Graves
on the Outer Banks*

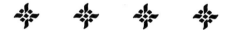

BY L. VANLOAN NAISAWALD

JOHN F. BLAIR, *Publisher*
Winston-Salem, North Carolina

Copyright © 1972 by JOHN F. BLAIR, *Publisher*
Library of Congress Catalog Card Number: 72–76481
ISBN 0–910244–65–0

Manufactured in the United States of America
by Heritage Printers, Inc.
Charlotte, North Carolina

CONTENTS

ILLUSTRATIONS

INTRODUCTION

OFF THE NORTH CAROLINA mainland lie the several long, finger-shaped islands known as the Outer Banks. For centuries these islands and their few hundred families lived in virtual isolation from the rest of America. Until the 1920's the only contact with the mainland was by boat across the wide sounds of Currituck, Albemarle, and Pamlico. Life was hard, but the Outer Bankers would have no other. Father and son, for generations, lived and died to the sound of the winds and the pounding of the sea, rarely, if ever, seeing as many as a hundred people together at one time. Most of the Bankers made a thin but satisfying living from the sea as fishermen or as Coast Guardsmen.

The seemingly endless stretch of dunes, the coves, and the stunted green forests of the Outer Banks are the sites of events inexorably a part of American history—Sir Walter Raleigh's Lost Colony, the exploits of pirates such as the infamous Blackbeard, and the first flight of a powered aircraft by Wilbur and Orville Wright. Here also, reaching from Wimble Shoals to Cape Hatteras, is "the Graveyard of the Atlantic," the treacherous waters, created by the head-on collision of cold and warm sea and air currents over the shifting shoals, that have proved so disastrous to coastwise shipping. In these waters, in two world wars, German submarines found a rich hunting ground and added their toll of sunken vessels to that of the storms.

As you drive through Ocracoke, the fishing village on the southern tip of the island of the same name, your curiosity is likely to be aroused by a small, neat white sign on the side of a winding lane that reads, in black stenciled letters, "British Cemetery." On investigating the four white stone crosses behind the white picket fence, you learn that these are the graves of four men of Britain's Royal Navy, killed off the Outer Banks in May 1942.

I first visited the cemetery in 1968. I was attracted and intrigued by the white, arrow-shaped sign, then captivated by the scene. I felt a sudden kinship with the men buried there, since the plaques on their crosses told me they had been recovered on the very day I had entered the U.S. Army from VMI. My curiosity was instantly aroused. What ship were they from? What had happened to them? Why were they buried here? Who had identified their bodies and how? Who maintains the little cemetery?

The long search to unravel the story took more than three years, and even so, some details, such as who was really the first person to find the bodies, are hidden forever in conflicting stories. This book is the result of my search. It is, first of all, the story of the British Cemetery, the men buried there, and their ship. But it is also the story of the deep affection felt by a group of Americans for the crew of an obscure little ship that scarcely rated being called a war vessel, though technically she was one.

Only a few people had ever heard of H.M.S. *Bedfordshire*, either in her home ports of Great Britain or in her temporary home in the United States. Her name would not find its way to the pages of World War II history books beside the names of such illustrious British men-of-war as H.M.S.'s *Hood, Prince of Wales, Exeter,* and a score of others whose sheer size and flaming heavy guns earned them a place on a printed page. But she earned a different kind of memory—a most warm and personal one in the hearts of the people of North Carolina's Outer Banks—and her memorial is the small four-grave cemetery on Ocracoke Island, wherein one of her officers and three of her crew rest peacefully in the shade of overhanging live oak, juniper, and yaupon. The site is a spot beautiful in its simplicity, and the story of how it came into being is one of sorrow, of compassion, of kinship, of the appreciation one group of people felt for another they had never met. But the common bonds of the sea and of ancestry between the British seamen and the islanders of Ocracoke probably ensure that there will always be this warm feeling for the cemetery.

I began my research with the knowledge that, since one was an officer, the men had come from a British war vessel; the gun crews on British merchant ships were normally headed by noncommissioned officers. A check of sinkings in David Stick's fine book, *The Graveyard of the Atlantic,* revealed only one such sinking within the time frame— H.M.S. *Bedfordshire,* an antisubmarine trawler operationally on loan to the United States Navy. From British authorities, I obtained data on her size, armament, and crew strength, and I learned that postwar investigation had revealed that she had been sunk by the *U-558* on a certain date and at a presumed position. From U.S. Navy archives, I was able to gain extracts of the captured log of the *U-558*, giving precise details of the torpedoing of the *Bedfordshire*, and from both the U.S. Navy and the Royal Canadian Navy, I was able to piece together parts of her voyage from the United Kingdom to the Carolinas and some of her activities during the period March–May 1942. German archivists and historians aided in the research and assisted in locating survivors of the *U-558*.

But the warm, human aspects of the story came from a handful of people who knew the ship or some of her crew, who recovered the bodies and helped bury them, and who maintain a fond guardianship over the cemetery. Foremost among those who provided many of the leads and much of the human aspect of this story is Aycock Brown of Manteo, North Carolina. Without his remarkable memory and his willingness to give of his time and to allow me access to his files, many of the details of the story would never have been learned. Also of great help were Miss Fannie Pearl Fulcher of Raleigh and Ocracoke, Wahab Howard, Harvey Wahab, and Jack Willis of Ocracoke, and Arnold Tolson of Manteo. Their roles in the events were first-hand and are vital to the successful and accurate telling. Each led me into an untold aspect of the story; one led to the discovery of the photograph of Lieutenant Cunningham taken two days before his death by S. S. Stevenson of Henderson, North Carolina.

But above all, considerable credit must go to that gallant lady, Mrs. Barbara Cunningham, wife of Lieutenant Cunningham, who gave me more of her time and thoughts than I had the right to ask or expect. It is to her and to the families of the other crewmen of H.M.S. *Bedfordshire* that I most respectfully dedicate this story.

L. VanLoan Naisawald

Manassas, Virginia
January 31, 1972

CHAPTER I

The Gray Wolves Return

To MOST AMERICANS in early 1942, the agony of World War II was a remote thing. Mounting casualty lists were still in the future, though fortunately for the nation, no uniformed, armed Nazi or Imperial Japanese soldier would ever set foot on the soil of the continental United States. But the grim realities of war came home quickly to those who lived along the Atlantic coast.

When the war broke there were men still living along the Virginia-Carolina beaches who could recall vividly the flames of burning ships and the drifting wreckage wrought by a handful of 1918 German U-boats. Little did they know that this was but a relatively amateurish prelude to the ship-slaughter that Adolph Hitler's U-boats would bring to this same coast a generation later.

The Japanese attack on Pearl Harbor triggered Hitler into declaring war on the United States, to his mind another decadent democracy capable of manufacturing washing machines and automobiles, but of small military threat. After all, were not the Americans still equipping their nonprofessional-type army with cardboard tanks and galvanized pipe to resemble mortar tubes? True, the U.S. Navy had been a nuisance to him, for their "neutral" destroyers had been accompanying British and Canadian warships on convoy duty in the North Atlantic. Even so, Hitler had instructed his U-boat commanders to avoid the U.S. men-of-war, but confrontations were bound to occur, as they did in the cases of the U.S.S.'s *Greer*, *Kearny*, and *Reuben James*.

But by declaring war on 9 December, Adolph Hitler felt free to loose his U-boats against all American vessels wherever they might be. As he saw it, the major threat from America would be from her mobilized manufacturing base, and if the Germans kept their stranglehold on the British Isles and at the same time ravaged America's east coast shipping lanes, the United States would be a giant chained to its shores.

Submarine Admiral Karl Doenitz studied the problem; it was not as easy as it seemed. German U-boat strength was averaging, over the last six months of 1941, 33 boats at sea at any one time. This was far short of Doenitz's original goal of 300 operational U-boats, a goal which would have allowed 100 boats to be at sea at one time, another 100 refitting, and the remaining third moving to and from patrol. Contrary to public belief, Germany had started World War II with only about 56 operational boats. But Hitler's production people were promising him 20 new boats a month beginning in 1942, so there should be enough to handle the added requirements for American waters.

Admiral Doenitz thereupon drew up an offensive plan that extended from Halifax, Nova Scotia, to Cape Hatteras, North Carolina. The plan, called *Paukenschlag*, or Drum-roll, was to begin 14 January 1942. However, by the end of December 1941, Doenitz was able to free only six U-boats for his American campaign. His goal of large wolf packs hovering off the American coast was never achieved; initially Hitler made too many demands on the U-boat force—to guard Rommel's supply line in North Africa and to protect German forces in Norway, a requirement arising from an illusory idea that the Allies were getting ready to recapture that country. As determined from captured U-boat records, the number of submarines the Germans stationed in North American waters in the first few months of 1942 averaged between six and eight, operating usually on an individual basis.

Paukenschlag actually began a day earlier than planned, when a U-boat skipper couldn't resist the temptation to sink a British freighter off Cape Cod on 13 January 1942. What became known to the Germans as the Great American Hunting Season had begun. It would last about three hideous months before the Americans would be able to muster the strength and skill to drive off the U-boats. But for those boats that did reach American waters, the hunting was superb. Inexperienced and naïve, the Americans sailed boldly in normal shipping lanes, unprotected, often with little blackout or smoke discipline, and with their radio operators jabbering incessantly in the clear about positions, speeds, weather, and rendezvous points. Adding to the inexperience of the Americans at sea was the stubborn stupidity with which Americans ashore resisted attempts to black out their coastal towns and cities at night. The sky-glow from the well-lit streets and buildings of east coast cities provided a perfect background against which the night-prowling U-boats could silhouette their targets.

The hunting areas selected by the German U-boat command were extended to cover the waters outside the major ports such as New York, Norfolk, and Boston, and along the very vulnerable shipping lanes that ran from the mouth of the St. Lawrence River, past New York and Cape Hatteras, southward to the Gulf or to the Windward Passage. Feeder lanes from ports such as Charleston, Savannah, Wilmington, Baltimore, and the New England area kept the seaways full of ships. This strip of the Atlantic, extending roughly 250 miles seaward from the coastline, was one of the world's most congested shipping lanes. The United States, as well as much of the world, depended on the traffic that passed here to sustain life and commerce. Oil, iron, steel, bauxite, coal, lumber, sugar, cotton, coffee, and a myriad of other materials critical to a nation at war were moved in bulk by hundreds of coastal tankers, freighters, and tug-hauled barges. The port of New York alone, in November 1941, averaged fifty ship departures and arrivals daily.

To defend adequately all the shipping moving along the 2500-odd miles of coastline from Maine to New Orleans was simply beyond the U.S. Navy's physical capability, to say nothing of its experience in modern antisubmarine tactics. Admiral S. E. Morison, the U.S. Navy's historian of World War II, has stated that it is not possible to say precisely how many antisubmarine vessels of any size were available when the war began, but it was certainly only a handful. Further, there were no naval aircraft capable of searching out to sea, so the Army Air Force tried to fill the void with a handful of ill-suited aircraft and inexperienced crews. There was little that could be done to offer protection to shipping other than to divert those vessels with shallow enough draughts to shallower waters and canals where their routes permitted. But this was only a small help; it gave no succor to deeper-draught vessels. British experience had proved that a seagoing convoy without adequate protection was worse than no convoy at all, and with the United States Navy battered by the Japanese onslaught in the Pacific, and understrength to the task, in any event, of fighting a two-ocean war, the "adequate protection" could not yet be provided. The result was that the hardy merchant skippers simply had to make a run for it, trusting to seamanship, weather, and blind luck.

Luckily for the Americans, the Germans were not able to bring a heavy, concerted attack to bear in January, for there was little that could have been done to stop it except to cease all shipping completely. This was scarcely feasible; too much of the nation's life blood moved by water along those vulnerable coastal lanes. The railroads were already overburdened and straining under the sudden wartime load; no more could be put on them at the time. The sea shipments had to continue.

For the inhabitants of the Outer Banks, then, a grisly three months began. The quiet, deserted, picturesque beaches were soon almost incessantly cluttered, as wreckage of every description was tossed up by the pounding waves.

There was never any doubt whence the debris had come; pieces of clothing, shattered and splintered deck planking, crates and bundles of floating cargoes, and great oozing smears of dark oil—the blood of dead ships—stained the sands, making a walk along the edge of the surf an in-and-out endeavor to avoid stepping into the dirty mess. And of course there were the even grimmer reminders, the bodies in the surf.

With the sudden transition from peace to war, the Outer Banks were not immune to a heavy rash of rumors of subversive activities. The navy's intelligence files reflect that their agents, in company with FBI men, were kept busy running from one part of the coast to another, checking out the flood of reports. It was reported that a man in Swansboro, North Carolina, was making suspicious trips to lonely Bear Island near Bogue Inlet, supposedly for the purpose of contacting German submarines or supplying them with fuel or provisions; that certain oil dealers were smuggling oil from eastern Carolina ports out to U-boats; that strange signal lights were flashing over a water tower near Manteo. Countless other reports of "suspicious activity" kept the agents chasing up and down the Carolina coast. But in no case were they able to confirm any subversion; usually the reports were from well-intentioned citizens whose newly war-jangled nerves had let their imaginations mislead them.

War really came to the Carolina coast on the night of 18 January 1942, when a U-boat drew first blood. Sixty miles off Cape Hatteras, the tanker *Allen Jackson*, loaded with nearly 73,000 tons of oil, was suddenly blown apart by two torpedoes. Instantly fire was everywhere. Twenty-two of thirty-five crewmen perished before the destroyer U.S.S. *Roe* arrived next morning to pick up survivors. The sixty-mile distance from shore precluded the sound of the explosion from being heard or the flames being seen from the beaches of the Outer Banks. But with news of the sinking, a number of "old-timers" on the beach undoubtedly recalled 16 August 1918.

On that day the British tanker *Mirlo*, carrying a full cargo of gasoline from New Orleans to Norfolk, hit a U-boat-laid mine off Wimble Shoals Light Buoy. Shortly thereafter her cargo of gasoline went up, and she was doomed. The explosion was seen by the lookout on duty in the now inactive Chicamacomico Coast Guard Station, seven miles northwest of the buoy, and one of the many feats of heroic rescue-at-sea by Outer Bankers followed. Station Captain John Allen Midgett and his boat crew rescued forty-two of the fifty-two men aboard the *Mirlo*, despite raging flames, gale winds, and heavy seas. There had been a few earlier sinkings, and two more would follow, but probably none had the personal impact on the Bankers that the sinking of the *Mirlo* had, and its memory lingered the most vividly.

Now, twenty-four years later, the horror was starting all over again, and this time the intensive three-month onslaught would make the World War I attacks seem insignificant by comparison. Following the sinking of the *Allen Jackson*, two more cargo ships went down that same day before the torpedoes of the sub or subs lurking off Hatteras. A fourth was sunk the next day, and the toll began its steady climb—a climb that would reach its crescendo in March and April 1942. Sinking records and U-boat logs for this period are incomplete, but it appears that eleven or twelve ships went to the bottom off the Outer Banks in January 1942, but probably not more than three at any one time. Wartime security withheld much information from the Outer Bankers as to shipping and submarine activity, and most of the actual sinkings were too far out to be seen and heard. Yet, often within a day or so, the Bankers knew from the flotsam the ocean currents and tides carried ashore that a U-boat had struck again. Frequently, rescuing ships would unload exhausted, shaken, and burned survivors at one of the Coast Guard stations such as that at Ocracoke, or at one of the larger naval bases such as that at Morehead City, and the whispered message of another sinking passed from person to person, from Cape Lookout to Norfolk.

It was against the rekindled glow of burning ships off the American east coast that the Navy Department realized the full magnitude of the German threat and the paucity of its own resources. There were simply not enough navy and Coast Guard patrol vessels and aircraft available. Until America's immense production capability was turned around to produce war materiel, anything that could be borrowed to help protect the coastal shipping lanes must be used. Time was the essential commodity; time had to be bought somehow—time to build new ships and aircraft, time to train crews, and time to organize an effective antisubmarine effort.

Hundreds of private yachts were taken into service, and along with other miscellaneous craft, they were converted into weakly armed patrol vessels. But a more likely source of help seemed to be the Royal Navy, because it had fought the sub threat in home waters earlier in the war. In early January, then, the U.S. Navy asked the British for assistance. In the course of the discussions, someone in Washington learned that there were forty PBY Catalina flying boats at Elizabeth City, North Carolina, which had been built for the British and were awaiting ferrying instructions to the United Kingdom. Perhaps His Majesty's government might release these planes to the United States. An inquiry was made but received an unfavorable answer. The British felt that their urgent need for these planes transcended that of the Americans. But, to provide a degree of help, they would be willing to loan the U.S. Navy a flotilla of twenty-four antisubmarine trawlers, which they had used earlier in the home waters fight and which seemed suitable for coastal patrol. The desperate Americans readily accepted the offer. The little ships would help to buy the needed time.

H.M.S. *Bedfordshire* was one of these ships. But it would be mid-February before she would sail from Britain with her sister trawlers, and the earliest the Americans could expect them would be early March. As it turned out, this expectation was far too optimistic; the Americans would have to fight alone and suffer appalling losses until April, when the refitted trawler fleet would begin to make its presence felt. In the meantime the battle would rage on, with the edge heavily in favor of the U-boats.

February 1942 was a light month in comparison with what was yet to come; only nine vessels went down off the Carolina coast. Nonetheless, the total of January and February had already passed the total of fifteen ships that the Germans had run up for all of 1918. Then came March. On the very first day the schooner *Anna R. Heidritter* was lost, not to enemy action but by running aground off Ocracoke. There was then a brief pause—the pause before the storm that came in the form of what was certainly a fresh set of U-boats in greater numbers. The tempest began when a tanker, the *Chester Sun*, was sent to the bottom on 10 March, and on the next day another U-boat nailed the *Caribsea* off Cape Lookout.

From the sinking of the *Caribsea* came one of the Outer Banks' most often-told legends of the war. The second mate of the ship was James Baugham Gaskill, whose birthplace was listed as Ocracoke. His parents ran a small inn that catered to sport fishermen, hunters, and vacationing celebrities, and Gaskill spent his youth on the shores of Ocracoke before going to sea as a young man. According to the tale that Ocracokers will tell you, Gaskill's mate's license had been in a wooden framed glass case displayed prominently on a cabin wall of the *Caribsea*, as is common with the licenses of most merchant officers. Gaskill did not survive the sinking, but the legend says that a piece of the cabin bearing young Gaskill's framed license drifted ashore on the ocean side of Ocracoke and was recovered by his cousin. Then, the next day, a wooden spar, supposedly carrying the name CARIBSEA, was recovered by a islander on the sound side of Ocracoke at the dock where the Gaskills' Pamlico Inn stood. The story goes on that Homer Howard of Ocracoke, whose ancestors were among the earliest settlers of the Island, took the spar and from it made a wooden cross bearing a small inscription telling of its origin. The unique little cross still stands on the altar of the Ocracoke Methodist Church.

That March a total of twenty-five vessels were destroyed, twenty-three of them in the last twenty days of the month. The slaughter continued into April at virtually the same pace. In the first eleven days, two cargo vessels and nine tankers fell to the U-boats. One of the tankers was the British *San Delfino*, torpedoed and set afire off Chicamacomico of *Mirlo* fame. Twenty-eight men perished when their lifeboat drifted into a mass of burning fuel. The bodies of several other members of her gun crew subsequently washed ashore and were turned over to U.S. Naval authorities for identification.

The grisly toll for April was twenty ships, not quite as bad as March, but more than the Allied merchant fleet could endure. The trend had to be reversed. Actually, administrative steps had been taken in February 1942, but it would be three more months before there would be significant results. Among the steps taken had been the creation of a special antisubmarine warfare command to handle the coastal shipping problem. One step the command took in April was to organize a system of "bucket brigade convoys." In the absence of sufficient escort vessels to send the shipping to sea in formal convoys, a partial convoy system was organized whereby groups of ships moved in daylight, as close to the shore as possible, from one anchorage to another, progressively up the coast, escorted by such local craft as were available from the various naval districts. At night, the preferred U-boat hunting time, these "bucket brigades" took shelter in protected anchorages roughly 120 miles apart, or a day's steaming distance. In some cases there were available harbors; in others, particularly south of Cape Henry, Virginia, the anchorages had to be net-protected areas. One of these net anchorages was established at Cape Lookout. But the system was not the full solution, which would not be found until sufficient strength, skill, and technology were combined in May 1942, thanks in no small measure to the British trawlers that had begun operations the month before.

CHAPTER II

H.M.S. *Bedfordshire*
Takes Station

IN EARLY FEBRUARY 1942, the little flotilla of antisubmarine trawlers, manned mostly by hardy British ex-
merchant seamen, set sail from England for the United
States. G. J. Y. Thorpe, VRD, RNR, of Lowestoft, England, the first lieutenant of one of these ships, the *Lady
Elsa*, remembers the trip was a rough, stormy one. The
ships carried 180 to 200 tons of coal—enough for eighteen
days' steaming—and Thorpe's vessel reached Nova Scotia
with 10 tons left in her bunkers. One trawler, the *Northern
Princess*, was lost in the heavy seas that seemed to bar their
way to the New World.

Comments in the message files in U.S. Navy archives
for January and February reflect the anxious waiting that
preceded news of the fleet's arrival. Where were they? Had
anyone heard from them? When could they be expected
to arrive? The war diary entries still show the urgency
with which the navy awaited help.

H.M.S. *Bedfordshire*, skippered by Lieutenant R. B.
Davis, RNR, and with a crew of three additional officers
and thirty-three men, was typical of her sister trawlers.
She had been built in 1935 at Middlesborough, England,

H.M.S. *Bedfordshire*

as a seagoing commercial fishing vessel, and along with hundreds of other trawlers, she had been taken over by the Royal Navy at the outbreak of war in 1939 and armed and equipped for antisubmarine duty in the western approaches to the British Isles. She was a sturdy vessel, though small as warships go—some 900 tons gross displacement and 170 feet long, or about a quarter of the size of a World War II destroyer. She was armed with a four-inch quick-fire deck gun, mounted forward atop an elevated platform, which had been added just aft of her bow, and a .303 caliber Lewis machine gun. But the most formidable part of her armament was the large supply of depth charge rails and launchers at her stern. The *Bedfordshire* was capable of carrying between 80 and 100 depth charges, and by using the two throwers on each side plus the rails off the stern, she could drop a pattern of ten charges. Some trawlers were also equipped with ASDIC, an early and not-too-reliable version of the antisubmarine detection device that relies on reflection of sound impulses off submerged bodies. According to Commander Thorpe, the usual tactics were for the trawlers to patrol in pairs, and the *Bedfordshire* had been the patrol leader of his group.

The *Bedfordshire* then, like all her sister vessels, could give a U-boat a very bad time. Her only disadvantage was her lack of speed. The triple expansion steam reciprocating engine, with which these ships were generally powered, developed between 800 and 1000 horsepower, but the top speed was rarely in excess of twelve knots, considerably less than that of a surfaced U-boat.

The hard-pressed Americans waited anxiously as the *Bedfordshire* and her sister vessels battled their way across the stormy North Atlantic. The February war diary of the U.S. Navy's Eastern Sea Frontier noted apprehensively that the ships were supposed to have sailed by mid-February for St. Johns, though by the end of the month, the Americans had had no word of their arrival. However, the ships must have reached Newfoundland very close to that time, for Canadian naval records reveal that the *Bedfordshire* left St. Johns, Newfoundland, on 5 March, in company with H.M. trawlers *Kingston Ceylonite* and *Norwich City*, headed for Halifax, Nova Scotia. En route to that port, the *Bedfordshire* picked up the survivors of the Norwegian motor vessel *Tyr*, which had been torpedoed and sunk by the *U-196* on 9 March off Nova Scotia, and on 11 March she put into the harbor at Halifax and landed the rescued seamen.

In the harbor, as the *Bedfordshire* arrived, was H.M.S. *Queen of Bermuda*, a former luxury liner that had been converted to an armed merchant cruiser. The *Queen*'s career had been short; she had run aground early in January 1942 and had had to return to port with serious damage—so serious that she needed to be towed to New York if repairs were to be made. But the lack of sufficient escort for a towed, vulnerable target of her size had kept her in Halifax harbor. Now, with the arrival of the *Bedfordshire* and four other trawlers—H.M.S.'s *Coventry City*, *Kingston Ceylonite*, *Lady Elsa*, and *Stella Polaris*—a solution was at hand. On 23 March the *Queen*, towed by a tug and escorted by the five trawlers, cleared Halifax for New York.

It was 31 March when the little convoy steamed up the East River toward the Brooklyn Navy Yard. Disappointment in their condition was clearly evident in the diary entries. The ships were all in bad need of overhaul; they were totally unsuited to operate in a southern climate; there was "not so much as a small pipe threading tool with which to make repairs"; and with two exceptions, they required a very high grade of coal to operate at an acceptable degree of efficiency. Where the overhauling, if any, took place is not mentioned, though if anything was done, it was probably at the Navy Yard. Thorpe still recalls the shock the Britishers experienced when they saw the Americans slapping a thick coat of blue-gray paint on the lovely white teak decks of the vessels. They would spend the next year or so trying to remove it.

How long the *Bedfordshire* stayed in New York the records do not show, but one recorded incident exists that attests to her stay in that port. The presence of uniformed British and other Allied sailors on the streets of New York City was becoming commonplace by this time, and groups of citizens and church organizations tried to dispel the loneliness felt by foreign servicemen in a strange city by offering the warmth of their homes. So it was that Mr. and Mrs. Francis Rycroft of Teaneck, New Jersey, British-born residents of America, opened their home to crew members of the *Bedfordshire*. One young lad, Wireless Telegrapher Stanley R. Craig, made a lasting impression on the Rycrofts, who kept a logbook of the signatures of all their visitors. One minor event involving Craig always helped recall him to their memory. One night after young Craig and his companions had left the Rycroft home and returned to the Brooklyn Navy Yard, the Rycrofts discovered his identification tag hanging on their bathroom door. They immediately called the Yard, notified the authorities that they would be bringing the tag, then drove over from New Jersey. Craig met them at the gate to retrieve his tag. They would not see him again, but Mrs. Rycroft would always remember with great warmth the smiling Craig, whom she described as having the wit of Red Skelton mingled with the seriousness of Bob Hope.

By the end of March, the U.S. Navy reported that fourteen of the trawlers were ready. The hard-pressed Americans eagerly deployed the little vessels along the Eastern Sea Frontier, though just when the *Bedfordshire* and her companions left New York is not clear. The sinkings for March, according to naval records, had reached an average of 1.35 vessels per day.

By mid-April the Americans, aided by the British trawler fleet, were beginning to learn how to defeat the deadly, gray U-boats. Coastal shipping was now moving in convoys, protected by the trawler fleet and a variety of other armed escort vessels. Better security measures were being followed, and aircraft patrols were aiding the surface searches. First blood for the Americans came on 13 April when the U.S.S. *Roper* caught the *U-85* on the surface off Nags Head, North Carolina, hit her with a three-inch forward gun, then depth-charged her to the bottom. The depth of the ocean at that point was such that the navy concluded that divers could be sent down for the possible recovery of valuable intelligence data. The *Roper* stayed over the sinking site for a number of hours until relieved by the *Bedfordshire* about 8:30 on the morning after the sinking. The British vessel stayed in that area through 22 April, covering the navy's diving operations.

The *Bedfordshire*'s activities for the rest of April and early May were the usual endless hours of patrolling in various locations from Cape Lookout, North Carolina, to Norfolk, Virginia. On 26 April official records show her as joining H.M.S. *Kingston Ceylonite* in protecting the torpedoed but still floating merchant vessel, *Harry Sinclair*, off Lookout Shoals.

At some point in this time frame—a time that today cannot be precisely determined, but possibly during the period when the *Bedfordshire* was guarding the diving operations over the *U-85*, or perhaps in the days just prior to her final visit into Morehead City—the *Bedfordshire* put into the navy base at Norfolk. There then occurred one of the several eerie coincidences that make up the intriguing tale of the *Bedfordshire* and some of her crew. During the stay in Norfolk, two North Carolinians met two officers of the *Bedfordshire* in a restaurant in that city. Wahab Howard of Ocracoke, at that time manager of the Ocracoke Electric Power and Light Company, and a friend, Shanklyn Austin of nearby Hatteras, were in Norfolk on business. On this particular evening the two men entered a crowded restaurant for dinner. A table became available, and the two sat down, reviewed the menu, and ordered. Then Austin, recalling that he had to make a telephone call, rose from the table and went to a telephone booth. At that moment the two Royal Navy officers, dressed in khaki uniforms, entered the restaurant, looked about to see all but one of the tables fully occupied, the one momentarily occupied only by Howard. The two officers thereupon walked over and politely asked if they might join him. As the table would accommodate four persons, Howard graciously agreed.

Austin returned, and introductions were exchanged. One of the officers, Sub-Lieutenant Cunningham, wearing a full black beard, asked Howard if he were from Norfolk. Howard explained that he was from Ocracoke. Where was that? asked Cunningham. About twelve miles south of Hatteras, explained Howard. The mention of Hatteras recalled a known point to the two Britishers, who then told the Americans that they were working out of Morehead City. The usual conversational pattern of Do-you-know-so-and-so? followed, and the rest of the evening was spent in enjoyable dining and conversation among the four men, as they exchanged experiences and mentioned acquaintances in Morehead City.

During the course of the evening, Howard's attention was attracted to Cunningham's very unusual yellow-gold watch with a black leather band and his yellow-gold ring bearing, as Howard now recalls, an initial set in black onyx. Howard would hear again very shortly of the watch and ring.

About 11 P.M. the four men stood up, shook hands,

Sub-Lieutenant Thomas Cunningham, RNVR,
aboard H.M.S. *Bedfordshire*

wished each other luck, and left the restaurant, the Royal
Navy men to put back to sea and the two civilians to return
the next morning to the Outer Banks.

In late April an American citizen visited aboard the *Bedfordshire* in Morehead City, North Carolina, a base for
antisubmarine operations and the new home port for the
Bedfordshire. The visitor was Aycock Brown, a civilian

special investigator for the Office of Naval Intelligence. Brown's duties at this time entailed identification of personnel washed ashore or recovered at sea, as well as the collection and analysis of any intelligence gained from bodies and debris. He had recently had the task of identifying four bodies recovered from the surf above Nags Head as being from the British tanker *San Delfino*, torpedoed on 9 April off Cape Hatteras. Brown's superior officer had suggested that it would be most proper if some British flags could be obtained for use in the burial rites, as well as a pallbearer detail or firing squad from a British man-of-war. Since the *Bedfordshire* was known to be in port, he suggested to Brown that he pay her a visit.

Brown, dressed in khaki shirt and trousers, reached dockside about midmorning, showed his pass to the guard, and walked down the quay beside the tied-up *Bedfordshire* toward a gangway. A British seaman stood nearby as other men were loading large wicker baskets with coal and hand-carrying them aboard the *Bedfordshire*. Where was the officer of the deck? inquired Brown of the sailor. The man pointed to a young bearded officer on the ship. That's him, Lieutenant Cunningham. Brown climbed aboard and asked for Cunningham, who promptly came forward and introduced himself. The American presented his identification and explained his mission of seeking flags and a burial party.

Cunningham, a slightly built, good-looking, genial man of twenty-eight, whose full dark beard belied his age, was most happy to agree to the flag request. If Brown would follow him below to the wardroom, he would get the flags for him. Once in the comfortably but plainly furnished wardroom, the young Britisher suggested to Brown that perhaps he'd like to participate in an ancient British naval custom by partaking of an issue of rum. When Brown accepted, Cunningham produced a large wicker-wrapped demijohn from which he poured two drinks. Each man in His Majesty's Naval Service, explained Cunningham, was entitled to a daily rum ration; for those who were non-drinkers, a small corresponding increase in pay was given.

The two men talked easily together for some time. Cunningham told Brown that he had graduated from college several years earlier with a science degree and had taught since then at a technical college. He had met his wife Barbara on their first day at Liverpool University, and they were married on 7 December 1940, when both were twenty-six years of age. Young Cunningham then proudly told the American that he and his wife were expecting an heir in October. By coincidence, both his skipper, Lieutenant Davis, and he had received similar news on the same day. Another series of drinks followed, and the American noticed that the demijohn was now empty. Since he had taken a fancy to the unusual container, Brown asked if he might have it as a souvenir. Most certainly, answered Cunningham, handing the empty jug to his new acquaintance. Feeling it was now time to go, Brown rose. Would a detail of crewmen be available for pallbearers at the funeral of the *San Delfino* crewmen? Unfortunately not, answered the lieutenant, as the ship was to leave as soon as she was coaled

Aycock Brown, who as a Navy Special Investigator identified the bodies, is shown here holding the demijohn given him by Sub-Lieutenant Thomas Cunningham.

to resume her offshore patrol station. But he did hand Brown a bundle of six new Union Jacks, two more than Brown needed. The two men then shook hands, and Brown, with the flags under his arm and an empty rum jug in his hand, left the *Bedfordshire*, never to see her again. He would see Cunningham once more, but under tragic circumstances.

About 7 or 8 May the *Bedfordshire* returned to Morehead City, probably for a brief refueling call. At least, in the memory of one American who was in Morehead City on Saturday, 9 May, the vessel was in port on that particular day. S. S. Stevenson of Henderson, North Carolina, was walking along a street of Morehead City, headed toward his own private cabin cruiser, the *Triple-S*, docked not far away. En route he met two British officers wandering slowly down the street; Stevenson introduced himself and asked if they would care to join him for lunch on his boat. Both men readily accepted. They were Lieutenant Davis and Sub-Lieutenant Cunningham of the *Bedfordshire*. During the pleasant visit on the Stevenson yacht, several pictures were taken of the two officers, pictures that Stevenson carefully dated "Saturday, 9 May 1942."

Also during the *Bedfordshire*'s last visit to Morehead City, a visitor from Ocracoke saw and would later recall the bearded young British officer. Jack Willis, then nineteen years old, had come to Morehead City from Ocracoke with his father on a grocery-buying trip. In the course of their stay in the city, the two men entered a drugstore. Three British naval officers were already in the store, and the

This photograph was taken aboard a private yacht at Morehead City, North Carolina, two days before the *Bedfordshire* was torpedoed. Sub-Lieutenant Thomas Cunningham is on the left, and Lieutenant R. B. Davis, the *Bedfordshire* commander, is on the right. The unidentified woman was a friend of S. S. Stevenson, owner of the yacht.

buzzing sound of an electric razor attracted young Willis's attention. One of the officers, a bearded man, was playfully toying with the razor, pretending to be shaving off his luxurious black growth. Willis did not learn his name until he saw him again several days later in the Coast Guard Station at Ocracoke.

It was probably Sunday that the *Bedfordshire* threw off her lines, cleared Morehead City for the last time, and put to sea. Submarine activity off the coast for the past few days had been very low. A ship had been lost on 29 April off Cape Lookout, but not until 5 May was there another, this time off Oregon Inlet. On the next day, a sister trawler, H.M.S. *Senateur Duhamel*, got into trouble off Fort Macon, colliding with the U.S.S. *Semmes*, a destroyer, and was lost. But if it looked as if things had calmed down a bit, Lieutenant Davis and the officers of the *Bedfordshire* were under no illusion that things would be quiet, for they probably had earlier navy intelligence estimates that placed the assumed U-boat strength in the western Atlantic at ten to twelve boats.

Also, the *Bedfordshire* may well have received the intelligence of an encounter on 9 May between a U-boat and the Coast Guard cutter *Icarus*. While Cunningham and Davis were enjoying Stevenson's hospitality, the *Icarus*, patrolling off Cape Lookout on the afternoon of 9 May, had suddenly picked up with her sound gear an unidentified and mushy contact. The cutter was moving south at a speed of fourteen knots, and the contact was to her port quarter at about 1000 yards range. The operator kept watching, and the contact continued to be soft until it drew even with the cutter on the port side. As the cutter began to pass it, the contact suddenly became firm, and then simultaneously and with frightening suddenness, a heavy explosion was seen, felt, and heard by the crew of the *Icarus*, about 500 yards off her port quarter. Within seconds the *Icarus*'s general quarters gong was sending her crew scurrying to battle stations, with deck guns cleared for action, and depth charges readied.

While the *Icarus* did not know it at the time, she was encountering the *U-352* under Kapitanleutnant Hellmut Rathke, and the U-boat skipper had spotted the cutter astern of him and prepared to attack. The U-boat's wake had apparently confused the sound signal reflected back to the *Icarus*, giving Rathke time to try a shot at the cutter. He fired one bow tube, but the torpedo—probably an electric one—evidently malfunctioned and detonated prematurely, creating the explosion seen and heard by the *Icarus*. Rathke, with the element of surprise lost and the cutter now showing her teeth, chose to try to escape. The *Icarus*, however, smelled a kill and quickly swung back toward the point of explosion. The U-boat also had moved toward the spot where the torpedo had exploded, Rathke apparently believing that the turbulence of the water would help screen his presence from the *Icarus*'s sonar gear. However, the cutter picked up her track and let go a depth charge attack. The sub reeled under the pounding concussions; her attack periscope was smashed, and an officer in the conning tower was killed. The pounding continued; gauges shattered, electric circuits went out, and men were thrown violently about. But the *U-352* remained alive. The *Icarus* then turned back for a second attack. This time the pounding was too great. The U-boat's vital electric motors were knocked out. Her skipper then decided that, with no ability to maneuver or to see, he would surface, save the crew, and scuttle the damaged U-boat. Rathke gave the order to blow her tanks, and the *U-352* started toward the surface.

As soon as the conning tower of the U-boat broke water it was the instant target for the *Icarus*'s deck guns. Thirty-three Germans were able to climb through the hatch under a hail of bullets and leap into the water. The gray boat stayed afloat for about four minutes before she plunged to the bottom, 125 feet down, carrying two officers and twelve crewmen with her. As she went, Rathke's scuttling charges exploded. The *Icarus* ceased fire and recovered Rathke and another officer and thirty-one crewmen from the sea. The U.S. Navy had succeeded in killing its second U-boat in American waters, but in all else involving the *U-352*, it wasn't very successful. It attempted several salvage efforts on the *U-352*, but was forced to abandon the work when unexploded depth charges were found near the sub. The Germans proved stubbornly uncooperative in divulging any useful military information, though subsequent grillings led navy interrogators to conclude correctly that at least one other U-boat had been in the area with the *U-352*. Actually, there were probably four: the *U-352*, the *U-701*, the *U-558*, and one other.

The *U-558*

CHAPTER III

The *U-558* Against
the *Bedfordshire*

ABOUT THE TIME that the *Bedfordshire* was standing
guard at the navy's diving operations over the *U-85*
in April, another sub, the *U-558*, was throwing off her
docking lines and putting out to sea, her destination America. Her skipper and her crew were veterans, and the boat
was "well shaken down." She had been built by Blöhm and
Voss in Hamburg, outfitted at Kiel, and commissioned on 20
February 1941. This was her seventh war cruise. She was of
the type known as a VII C boat, of 770 tons, carrying four
twenty-one-inch bow torpedo tubes and one stern tube. She
had the capacity to carry fourteen torpedoes. To provide
surface action and antiaircraft defense, the *U-558* carried
a 3.5-inch gun forward and a light antiaircraft cannon aft.
Her normal crew was forty-four officers and men. She was
the principal type of U-boat employed by Germany in
World War II.

Kapitanleutnant Gunther Krech, her skipper, had been
born on 21 September 1914, in Wilhelmshaven, from
which so many of Germany's naval families came. He had
entered the naval academy in 1933. His terse biographical
sketch in captured German naval records shows that he

Gunther Krech (eighth from left) as First Officer of the *U-100*

had attended training courses in 1939–40 before becoming first officer of the *U-100* from May 1940 until November 1940. What went unsaid by this entry was that the *U-100* was commanded by Kapitanleutnant Otto Schepke, and Schepke in the *U-100* became one of Hitler's three greatest U-boat aces. Krech had had a good teacher. He had been given command of the *U-558* on her launching, and he was her skipper until her demise three years later.

Gunther Krech became something of a legend in the German submarine service, for he carried with him a sea-going aquarium. In this tank were pet fish whom he had named after crowned heads and prime ministers of the powers at war with Germany. Wilhelmina was a handsome goldfish; she met an unfortunate end when she fell from a spoon into the bilges while the aquarium was being cleaned. Churchill was a small temperamental pirate fish. He had made three patrols before he succumbed and was ceremoniously interred in an alcohol-filled glass tube, which was then suspended from the lamp in the wardroom.

The first two cruises of the *U-558* were uneventful; on the third she got her first ship. Her fourth cruise, in October 1941, was quite lively, for she caught up with a weakly escorted Britain-bound convoy 400 miles south of Iceland. In conjunction with several other U-boats, Krech attacked repeatedly. He sank one ship on 15 October, and then on 17 October he fired at a tanker but missed. However, the shot did find a target in another ship farther back in the convoy. Krech did not see the hit but heard the explosion. A second torpedo bagged another tanker for sure. Krech took a fast look through the periscope a few minutes later, and lo! another ship had stopped nearby, apparently picking up survivors. A quick range estimate and bearing, followed by the cry Fire! sent a third torpedo slamming into the stopped ship. A fourth shot bagged still another luckless vessel. Three more torpedoes he fired at fleeing targets without scoring, but for Gunther Krech and the *U-558*, it had been a very successful day.

But a disturbing radiogram was received the next day. The German High Command had learned authoritatively that the U.S.S. *Kearny* had been torpedoed and damaged by a submarine on 17 October! Where was he? What had he fired at? What did he identify? The questions came from an anxious Doenitz to all U-boat commanders in the area. Hitler had issued strict orders to avoid attacking American warships despite their active and often aggressive convoy assistance. Krech identified his targets as three tankers sunk, one steamer sunk, and one steamer probably sunk.

Nonetheless, from a quick review of American accounts of the *Kearny*'s action, it appears that Krech may have been the guilty party. The *Kearny*, along with four other U.S. destroyers, had responded to the convoy's call for help after the first of the U-boats scored three sinkings on 10 October. By 16 October they were on station when the wolf pack struck again. A torpedoed ship about 1200 yards from the *Kearny* burned brilliantly, providing a clear silhouette to the waiting subs. Suddenly, a corvette swept toward the *Kearny*'s bow, and the American skipper brought the destroyer to a stop to avoid collision. Before she could resume

34

speed, a torpedo smashed into her starboard side; causing heavy casualties. Hitler had drawn unintentional first American blood, probably via Gunther Krech.

By the time the *U-558* left Brest on 12 April 1942, she had six war cruises behind her, and her skipper would soon wear proudly the Knight's Cross of the Iron Cross for his hunting skill. This time she would join some sister U-boats off the American east coast. Experience had taught the Germans that their Class VII C boat had a longer range capability than they had originally believed. It would be 21 June before she would return to Germany, thanks to the newly discovered range and to the opportunity to join three other U-boats on 29 April west of the Azores in refueling and replenishing with seven days' supplies from one of Doenitz's new "milch-cows," torpedo-tubeless subs designed solely as resupply vessels.

For the first three days in May, the *U-558* patrolled fruitlessly off Bermuda. Krech thereupon decided to shift his patrol area northward, so on 4 May he set his course for Cape Hatteras. There he hoped to find an abundance of coastal shipping. He would also find that the days of the Great American Hunting Season were over.

On 5 May (6 May, German time) Gunther Krech noted in his log that he was east of Cape Lookout, and for the next three days, the *U-558* cruised back and forth between Capes Hatteras and Lookout. It was 1:15 on the afternoon of 8 May when Krech spotted in the distance his first potential quarry—a small convoy of seven tankers and cargo ships escorted by three war vessels. They appeared to be moving at a speed of eight knots and to be following the twenty-five-meter depth line. The German reluctantly concluded that the distance was too great for him to attack, but he planned to run on the surface in hopes of catching the convoy as it rounded Cape Lookout. He would then make a surface night attack; a daylight strike in these shallow waters was too risky.

The chase began. At 6:45 P.M., 9 May, a patrolling aircraft passed by but failed to notice the U-boat. But Krech had now lost the convoy. The men on the U-boat's sound listening gear strained in vain for propeller noises. Overcast skies and a growing fog forced Krech to move slowly on the surface, still hopeful of a contact. Shortly after midnight, Krech had to advise Doenitz's headquarters that he had lost contact and assumed the convoy was moving south along the twenty-meter line; he would continue searching. By early morning of 10 May the *U-558* was southeast of Frying Pan Buoy, a key navigation point about fifty miles southeast of Cape Lookout. Since there was such a narrow difference in speed between the U-boat and the convoy, Krech decided at 8:25 P.M. to give up the chase and try for a new quarry.

By 2:00 A.M. on 11 May, he was again southeast of Cape Lookout. The skies were overcast, but visibility was good. At 1:30 P.M. Krech ordered a practice dive—a frequent occurrence on patrols. Down went the *U-558*, her listening gear always alert. Suddenly, the German sailor manning the instrument called out a contact—260 degrees astern! Krech came to periscope depth, ran up the scope, and took a fast look. Two patrol vessels were clearly in view; furthermore, the Germans now heard the distinctive pinging of the British ASDIC as it searched the sea depths. Another look showed one vessel on a course of zero degrees, headed straight for him. Krech pulled the periscope and ordered the boat to dive for the bottom!

On the sea floor the crew of the sub prepared for the expected crash of depth charges. The Germans waited; the vessel passed slowly overhead and nothing happened. With a feeling of relief, they heard the noise of the propellers move slowly away. But Krech took no chances; he stayed put. Four hours later he heard four separate but distant detonations like depth charges, and his listening gear also picked up an impulse astern. About 5½ hours passed in all before the *U-558* came up to periscope depth again and her skipper swept the horizon with his scope. Though the sun was now setting, he picked up the outline of two patrol vessels, probably the same two he had encountered earlier.

Gunther Krech made a decision; he would wait another forty-five minutes, then surface his boat and make a run for it in the coming darkness. On the surface he could attain a speed of about eighteen knots—about twelve more than he could do submerged—and a speed of eighteen knots was faster than that of the twelve-knot patrol trawlers. Krech waited his three-quarters of an hour, then surfaced, pointed his boat south, and started away, generally following the coastline as he went.

It appeared to the German that he might make good with his scheme. A flashing white light off his stern, about forty minutes later, gave him a bit of concern, causing the lookouts on the sub's conning tower to be unusually alert in the moonless overcast night. Then, at 10:07 P.M., a ship's silhouette appeared off the sub's stern. A quick second look showed it was apparently a patrol vessel. Kapitanleutnant Krech, his mind probably keenly aware that he had no sinkings to show for his month at sea, promptly turned to attack the unsuspecting ship, using a surface attack—the preferred German sub tactic at this stage of the war.

Krech maneuvered his sub into a firing position. Through his attack periscope, he tracked the trawler. She was moving at about six knots and at a range of 1000 meters. The target data went to the fire direction plotters, and a torpedo course was established. At 11:26 P.M. Gunther Krech barked: Fire one! Fire two! With that he swung the sub away from the target and waited for the explosion. Five minutes passed—more than enough running time—but no explosion shook the night. Both torpedoes obviously had missed. But his target, H.M.S. *Bedfordshire*, gave no evidence of having seen the torpedoes pass or of having detected the sub's presence.

Krech maneuvered into a new firing position. This time the range was down to 600 meters! At 11:40 P.M. the German skipper commanded: Fire three! and once again turned away to await the hit. Clinging to the periscope, Krech waited. Seconds ticked by; at the count of thirty-six, a heavy detonation ripped the night open, and the German skipper saw the little vessel hit square amidships. Her stern rose high out of the water and plunged almost instantly from sight. Gunther Krech pulled down his scope, made the entry in his log, and resumed his southward course. To U.S. Naval Headquarters along the Eastern Sea Frontier, there was apparently no news from the *Bedfordshire* of any activity prior to the attack, only a routine message, time-dated "2012Z11May," or 3:12 that afternoon. So far as navy sources knew, the *Bedfordshire* was still on patrol, as ordered, between buoy four, 34°53' north latitude, 75°31' west longitude, and buoy fourteen, 34°18' north latitude, 76°24' west longitude. But the German U-boat captain gave the position at the time of sinking by a coded grid square that the British Admiralty later interpreted as 34°10' north latitude, 76°41' west longitude.

Hatteras Inlet

Pamlico Sound

Ocracoke Island

The Knolls

Spot where
Tolson found the
first body

Ocracoke
Village

Spot where second body
was found

Scale

0   1   2   3   4   5000 yds.

Ocracoke
Village

Ocracoke
Village

Site of Gaskill
Pamlico Inn

Lighthouse

National Park Service
Visitor Center

W. Howard
Res.

Howard-Wahab Cemetery

British Cemetery

J. P. Fulcher Residence

Methodist Church

School

Point where citizen
told Tolson of
second body

Airstrip

L. Gaskill
Residence

Silver Lake

CHAPTER IV

The Ocean Discloses the Fate

WHAT HAPPENED on the morning of 14 May 1942 is clouded in part by conflicting accounts and honest differences in memories. But according to the version the author accepts, a twenty-year-old Coast Guardsman named Arnold Tolson, a native of nearby Buxton, set out on a beach patrol early that morning from the Ocracoke Station in company with another young Coast Guardsman known to his mates as "Okie." Okie would be taking over this early morning patrol duty from Tolson, so the latter was showing him the route. About 6:00 A.M. the two men climbed into their Coast Guard truck, drove out onto the beach, and headed toward Hatteras Inlet. Their patrol would cover about half the distance; the other half would be the responsibility of the Hatteras Coast Guard Station.

It was about 7:00 A.M., and they were almost to the end of their drive up the wide, deserted beach when Tolson spotted something in the surf, which looked at first glance like a man waving, his arms flailing about. It couldn't be a swimmer, for there was no habitation anywhere near—only the desolate dunes, hiding the wild pony herd, and the endlessly pounding surf and sea.

A second look told Tolson that it was a body in the heavy surf. Stopping the truck, he jumped out, removed his shoes, and waded out into the lashing white waves. Though Tolson had lived on the Outer Banks all his life—indeed, he believed he was the youngest chief in the regular Coast Guard—and the Outer Bankers had a long and exemplary tradition of saving shipwrecked mariners and recovering bodies, this was Tolson's first meeting with a body in the surf.

With Okie's help Tolson put the fully clad body into the back of the truck, covered it with a canvas, and headed back toward the Ocracoke Coast Guard Station. As they neared the village, a local citizen flagged them to a stop. According to the prevalent version, this man was Elwood Austin of Ocracoke, who had been fishing on the point with his wife and a relative. Tolson stopped the truck; Austin told him there was a body in the surf, almost at the inlet. The Coast Guardsman thereupon turned his truck around, and the two men drove down toward the point, which was perhaps two miles down the beach, watching for the body as they drove. Then they saw it. Once again Tolson waded out, picked up the body, and carried it to the truck. With that, they turned back to the Coast Guard Station at Ocracoke village, where the chief in charge of the station, Homer Gray, took over.

The two bodies were carefully removed from the truck and placed in a small room in a little building at the back of the station—a room that had once been a kitchen, before the facility was expanded.* A tarpaulin was carefully

* This building was subsequently purchased by Wahab Howard and now stands behind his home in Ocracoke village, where Howard uses it as a workshop and for storage.

Chief Boatswain's Mate Arnold Tolson

placed over the two bodies, and Homer Gray telephoned naval headquarters in Morehead City of the event.

Shortly after Gray's message was received in Morehead City, Aycock Brown received his orders to get a marine am-

phibian aircraft from nearby Cherry Point and go to Ocracoke. It was noon or a little after when he arrived. He was
met by the Coast Guard chief, and the two men moved immediately to the makeshift morgue. Gray and Tolson then
tossed back the tarpaulin, exposing the fully clad bodies.

Brown instantly recognized the bearded face that gazed
up at him. "I know that man, from Morehead City. He's
off the *Bedfordshire*!" Though he was not wearing identification tags, the papers in his pocket confirmed Brown's
initial reaction; he was Sub-Lieutenant Thomas Cunningham, Royal Navy Volunteer Reserve. In the left sleeve of
his Royal Navy sweater, the officer had stuffed his sun-
glasses and a bankbook on a Morehead City bank. A Morehead City newspaper was still crammed in his hip pocket.
There was no visible cause of death.

Since regulations required that certain articles of clothing, as well as papers and personal effects, he removed from
recovered dead and forwarded to higher naval headquarters, the two men gently took off Cunningham's regulation
dark blue turtleneck sweater and his shoes and set them
aside with the papers and personal effects. The ring and
watch that had caught the eye of Wahab Howard in the
Norfolk restaurant would be returned to Cunningham's
wife shortly.

Turning then to the next body, the one recovered near
the inlet, Brown began to search the pockets, there being
no I.D. tags about this man's neck either. Once again papers
and a name in his skivvy shirt provided an answer; he was
Stanley Craig, Ordinary Telegraphist, Royal Navy. Fin-

gerprints taken by Brown at this time subsequently officially confirmed the identity. Charles L. Swindell, a local doctor, was asked to determine the cause of death. In the absence of any external wounds, the doctor concluded that the men had died by concussion or drowning or a combination of both. Gathering up the articles of the two men, Brown thereupon turned to the problem of prompt and proper burial, which was required by regulations as well as by custom on the morticianless Outer Banks.

At first Brown thought that the wartime shortage of lumber might pose a coffin problem, and he muttered this thought aloud. But the Coast Guard, true to its motto *Semper Paratus*, had already solved the problem. Two large, heavy wooden boxes had been found recently on the shore of Silver Lake, the clear bay about which clusters the village of Ocracoke. They were of rugged construction and were six to seven feet long. Shaped somewhat like coffins and called locally battery or sink boxes, they were used in prewar days by duck hunters. A hunter could lie flat on his back in such a box as it floated in the water, his decoys out on both sides, and as the hunted ducks approached, he could easily raise himself up and fire. Homer Gray recalled the presence of these boxes and suggested that they would make ideal coffins; yet their ownership was unknown. A query was made of the local postmaster, who in Ocracoke was a sort of high authority on all matters. It was his considered opinion that the boxes were abandoned property and, therefore, could be used for the purpose the Coast Guard had in mind. As a result, the two English friends of America received the very best the Americans could provide, which one might say surpassed that normally available for World War II battle deaths.

Next came the other details of the funeral. Since there was no ordained priest or minister available, Brown asked Amasa Fulcher, a lay leader of the only church on Ocracoke Island—the Methodist—to conduct the services. Since regulation prescribed that recovered deceased personnel could be given a Christian service and buried in private ground, the problem of a cemetery was solved by the generosity of the local Williams family. They readily donated land adjacent to their own family cemetery.

That same evening the two Britishers were gently wrapped in clean sheets and navy blankets and placed in the makeshift caskets. With a U.S. Coast Guard contingent in full uniform as pallbearers and the caskets draped with the two extra Union Jacks with which Cunningham had earlier provided Brown, the interment was carried out, even including the solo singing of a hymn by Fulcher. As Brown recalls today, "It was a typical Outer Banks funeral."

With all the required and proper details completed, Aycock Brown called his headquarters to report his findings. His headquarters questioned his reference to the men being from the *Bedfordshire*; they had had no distress call or report of an attack on the *Bedfordshire*. Brown replied that that might well be, but indeed he knew Cunningham was off that ship. "Wait a minute," came the voice over the phone. "I'll check again." Then, after a short wait, the voice sounded more sympathetic; the last word they had had from the *Bedfordshire* had been on 11 May, so maybe she had run into trouble. The navy continued to show her officially on station, however, until 16 May, at which time it acknowledged that she was missing in action and probably sunk.

Ocracoke was then, as it is now, a small village, and word of any unusual event spread rapidly. The morning the bodies were found, Wahab Howard was back in his office at Ocracoke after his visit of several days in Norfolk. A Coast Guard truck had stopped momentarily in front of his office, not an unusual event in a community whose people and heritage were vested in that service. Even when Howard heard someone mention that there were two bodies in the truck, just recovered from the beach, there was no reason for him to inquire further; the recovery of bodies from the restless sea of Ocracoke and Hatteras was not an altogether unusual event. Howard remained at his desk. But late that afternoon Howard met his cousin, Harvey Wahab, then a Coast Guardsman stationed with the Ocracoke unit. Any idea who the men were that were found this morning? asked Howard. No, replied Wahab, only that they were men of the Royal Navy. One of them, he said, had the blackest moustache he had ever seen. Howard's curiosity was aroused. Did he have a full goatee-type beard? Yes, he did. Howard was now quite sure that one was his friend of the Norfolk visit—Lieutenant Cunningham. He told Wahab of the meeting, of the fact that the man had been off the *Bedfordshire*, and of his association with Morehead City. It all ties in, said Wahab, as he told

47

his cousin of the finding of the Morehead City bankbook on Cunningham. What about the watch and ring that had caught Howard's eye? Wahab replied that the officer was still wearing them.

It was at this same time that Jack Willis also learned of the event and came to the station. There he saw the two bodies, one of which was his bearded friend of the electric razor incident.

A week passed. Arnold Tolson was now aboard the station's sixty-three-foot patrol boat, USCG *63-067*, on patrol about four or five miles northeast of Ocracoke Inlet. Suddenly two bodies were spotted in the water. As these were in bad condition and clad only in the same dark blue turtleneck sweaters worn by the *Bedfordshire*'s crew, a stretcher was lowered under each and the remains recovered.

Again the indefatigable Aycock Brown strove to make identification. But in this case there was no possible means. One could only conclude from the sweaters that they had been British seamen, probably from the *Bedfordshire*. But the official record would have to show "unknown."

The decision was then made to bury the two men in the cemetery with Lieutenant Cunningham and Seaman Craig. However, here again the paucity of lumber threatened to complicate Brown's task. According to one account, the Coast Guardsmen learned of a local resident who had some years earlier acquired a good supply of lumber with which to build a new outhouse. But for some reason, he had never got around to the task. Would he donate the lumber to this worthy cause? he was asked. An instant affirmative reply set saws and hammers to work. Still others insist that the lumber and labor were supplied by the T. A. Loving Company, which was engaged in building a naval installation on Ocracoke at the time. But whatever the source, lumber was provided, and the two unknown seamen were laid to rest.

In late June 1942, Brown went to the First-Citizens Bank and Trust Company of Morehead City to determine what disposition had been made of the account Lieutenant Cunningham had apparently had with that bank. The cashier replied that the fund, $155.00, was still on deposit, as were the deposits of Lieutenant Davis of $100.00 and of Sub-Lieutenant Bruce Hall of $60.00. There was also a deposit of $90.00 in the name of the Ward Room of the *Bedfordshire*. This information Special Agent Brown turned over to his superiors so that the British authorities could obtain release of the funds.

According to data now available, H.M.S. *Bedfordshire* rests on the bottom of the Atlantic, about forty miles southeast of Cape Lookout, in some 100 to 150 feet of water. The precise spot is unknown, but the British Admiralty gives the location as being 34°10′ north latitude and 76°41′ west longitude. Little was ever recovered that was positively identified as being from the trawler. A small wooden lifeboat came ashore some days afterward at Portsmouth Island, but Aycock Brown found nothing in it or on it to identify where it came from. However, some weeks after the tragedy, Brown happened to visit in the village of At-

49

lantic, twenty-five miles below Ocracoke, on the mainland. He recalls very vividly walking down a dock on a pressing errand and noticing a long white board, perhaps fifteen feet in length, resting on the dock where the mailboat normally tied up. On the board in black letters was the name BEDFORDSHIRE. It was a nameboard off the ship, and it had washed ashore near the now-closed Coast Guard Station at Core Banks opposite Atlantic.

At the suggestion of Brown, the author addressed letters to several persons in Atlantic who might possibly have knowledge of the whereabouts or fate of the nameplate, but no answer was ever received.

On the morning of the recovery of Cunningham's and Craig's bodies, a flagstaff and Union Jack were found, along with a pair of German Zeiss binoculars, in the surf at Ocracoke. Wahab Howard found the binoculars and Lum Gaskill and two others found the staff and flag. Gaskill still retains the staff, but says that he gave the Union Jack to the burial party, who wrapped Cunningham's body in it. This may be true, though Tolson, Gray, and Brown maintain they wrapped the two men in sheets and U.S. Navy issue blankets and do not recall using a flag other than those furnished by Brown to cover the caskets.

The photograph of H.M.S. *Bedfordshire* provided the author by Cunningham's widow clearly shows a flag flying from a mast on the stern of the *Bedfordshire*. Unfortunately, it cannot be determined if the flag is the Union Jack or the beautiful white ensign. According to authorities at the British Naval Attaché's office in Washington, D.C., normal practice would have been for a British war vessel to be flying the white ensign—a flag with a white background, intersected by the red cross of St. George, with the Union Jack in the upper left field. The Union Jack was normally flown only in port. As to whether the flag and staff found by Gaskill were off the *Bedfordshire*, one cannot say for certain. The author examined the staff and all that could be learned from it was that it was of marine type, of hard wood, about eight feet tall, about four inches in diameter, with a large wooden knob at the top that housed two halyard pulleys. It was obviously a flagstaff of the type and size that one might expect to find on a wooden-decked merchant vessel or a trawler such as the *Bedfordshire*.

The Memorial Service, 27 December 1942

CHAPTER V

The British Cemetery
Becomes Permanent

IN OCTOBER 1942 Lieutenant Cunningham's attractive
wife Barbara gave birth to a son, whom she named Thomas after his father. Earlier that fall she had written a letter
to the British naval authorities in America asking if a Roman Catholic priest had conducted the burial service, since
her husband had been a devout Roman Catholic. In September, the inquiry reached the desk of Lieutenant Commander Alan D. Bruford of the British Trawler Office
in Norfolk. Commander Bruford forwarded the letter
through U.S. Navy channels, and in time it reached Aycock
Brown. Brown turned the letter over to Amasa Fulcher,
who had conducted the funeral services. In view of Mrs.
Cunningham's concern, it was decided to try to conduct a
special memorial service with a Roman Catholic navy chaplain from Cherry Point Marine Air Station in attendance.
Fulcher, believing that a woman's touch might be more
appropriate, asked his young schoolteacher daughter if she
would undertake to reply to Mrs. Cunningham. Out of
this reply by Fannie Pearl Fulcher, now a retired teacher
of Raleigh and Ocracoke, North Carolina, has grown a

long and fond friendship between her and the Cunningham family.

Brown seems to have been a driving force in the preparation of the memorial service. For example, Brown found that the graves had fallen into disarray, so a plea was made to the commanding officer of the new U.S. Navy Section Base on Ocracoke for help. This officer responded by having the area cleared of brush and vines, by erecting white wooden crosses, and by making the military arrangements for a service with a Catholic chaplain.

At 1:30 P.M., 27 December 1942, a navy bugler sounded Assembly, and a long line of U.S. Navy and Coast Guardsmen fell into position. The uniform was Blues with white hats. At a shouted command the column moved out, the bugler leading, followed by Lieutenant Commander Donald Strange, the Roman Catholic chaplain, and the Reverend W. R. Dixon, pastor of the local Methodist church. Then came the detachment of officers in Dress Blues with side arms; the firing squad in white hats, leggings, and webbed belts came next. They were followed by a large body of chief petty officers and enlisted personnel from the navy base and the Coast Guard Station at Ocracoke.

On reaching the cemetery the officers formed on the left side facing inward, the firing squad took position on the right side, and the remainder of the escort formed behind the firing party. Dixon stepped forward and led the Protestant burial service. Minutes later Chaplain Strange performed the Roman Catholic rites. As Chaplain Strange closed his book and stepped back, the formation came to

55

Present Arms. Then came the crash of the traditional three volleys, signifying the Trinity, quickly followed by the navy bugler sounding Taps. As the last note faded, the arms were grounded and the formation prepared to move back to barracks.

At some later date, in 1943, Commander J. J. Wilkinson, Commanding Officer of the Ocracoke Section Base, along with Agent Brown, took renewed interest in the grave site and directed personnel of his command to clear the area of brush again and to erect a white picket fence around the four graves. Prior to November 1943, according to an official letter of Brown's to his superior dated that month, the wooden crosses had been replaced with stone markers to which bronze identification plates were attached. The markers were donated by the T. A. Loving Company. These are unquestionably the same markers that are present today, and they are in the same positions as their wooden predecessors. The stones marking the graves of the two unknown sailors are dated erroneously 14 May 1942. Their bodies were not recovered until the following week.

The author, along with several others close to the story, had until recently a lingering doubt as to whether the headstones corresponded to the actual graves. The primary reason for such a question was that Cunningham and Craig, who were recovered, identified, and buried on the same day, were apparently buried diagonally to each other, a superficially illogical pattern. Would it not have been more logical to bury the men side by side or head to toe?

According to Arnold Tolson, who was a member of the

burial party, the Coast Guardsmen dug two graves "side by side" in land donated by the Williams family. Tolson himself had taken the detail to the burial site, started them digging on the first grave, and then returned to the station. He did not return until the burial later that day and did not recall who was placed on the right.

However, the "side by side" theory was contested by certain Ocracokers. According to Wahab Howard, the graves were dug head to foot and parallel to the Williams cemetery because of the heavy brush and trees close to the cemetery fence. The detail therefore felt that the easier and more appropriate way to dig the two new graves was to clear a narrow strip of brush and trees parallel to the Williams plot rather than a wider strip at the rear that would have left a wall of brush in front of the two graves. Efforts to confirm this in 1971 from another ex-Coast Guard Ocracoker who was present at the time, Harvey Wahab, seemed only to confuse the picture. Wahab, a cousin of Wahab Howard, said that he also participated in the burial—his presence has been confirmed by a photograph—and that Craig was buried on the left front as one faces the cemetery, with Cunningham on the right and the two subsequent "unknowns" to their rear. As it turns out his memory was partially correct.

The next two bodies were recovered approximately a week later; the records do not reflect the exact date, but Tolson and Brown agree that it was "about a week later," and contemporary records retained by Brown confirm the interval as being "about a week." These two bodies, like the bodies of Cunningham and Craig, were interred the day they were recovered in the same plot of ground donated by the Williams family. Tolson did not recall, in 1969, whether these two graves were in front of, behind, or alongside those of Cunningham and Craig, but he did recall that again the two were buried "side by side."

That the four graves went unmarked from May until approximately November or early December 1942 is evident from an official letter, a copy of which was dated 27 December 1942 and was retained by Brown. It contains the following:

When the new commanding officer of the Section Base [Ocracoke] learned that the bodies were buried here he cooperated with this Agent [Brown] in obtaining permission to clear up the cemetery of bushes, erecting white crosses to mark the graves. . . .

The photographs of the 27 December memorial service show clearly four things: (1) the four graves are marked with fresh wooden crosses; (2) the ground about the four graves is clean and clear of bushes and brush; (3) the wooden crosses are placed so that Cunningham's and Craig's graves are not side-by-side nor head-to-foot; and (4) the crosses are at the foot and not at the head of the graves, in a position they also appear to be today. These four facts are in accord with the theory that the graves were probably unmarked for five months, as indicated by Brown's letter, and that once the decision was made to hold a memorial service to abide by Mrs. Cunningham's request, personnel from the newly constructed naval base at Ocracoke cleaned

The burial of Thomas Cunningham, 14 May 1942. Chief Boatswain's Mate Harvey Wahab is in the right foreground, and Arnold Tolson (with tattoo on arm) is on the left. Stanley Craig's grave can be seen behind Tolson.

the area and made the wooden crosses, and a detail of sailors hurriedly placed them at the foot of the mounds.

Two possibilities seemed most clear. First, that the two graves at the back or north end of the cemetery were the first two—those of Cunningham and Craig—since they are on a line with the back edge of the adjacent Williams cemetery, and that the grave on the left rear as one faces the cemetery was that of Cunningham, the senior man, with Craig buried on the right. This would have meant an arrangement as follows:

Cunningham	Craig
Unknown	Unknown

The second possibility, and the one the author originally felt was probable, was that the two left-hand graves were those of Cunningham and Craig, while the right-hand ones were those of the two unknown sailors.

The question remained an open, nagging one until the very final moments before the publication of this book. Then Aycock Brown discovered in his papers a yellowed contemporary photograph of the interment of Lieutenant Cunningham. The legend he had appended to it reads as follows:

This Union Jack drapes the coffin of S/Lt. Thomas Cunningham at the burial rites conducted on Ocracoke Island. Cunningham's body came ashore on the island about two or three weeks after he had loaned the same Union Jack to Naval Intelligence Agent Aycock Brown who wanted it to use in draping the coffin of another British subject whose body had washed ashore near Cape Hatteras.

In forwarding the photograph to me, Brown called attention to the apparent diagonal location of two graves. A very large enlargement was made, and it discloses beyond much doubt the existence of two graves *at a diagonal to each other*. The first is directly in the foreground and is labeled by Brown as Cunningham's. The mound of excavated earth can be seen clearly on the right of the photograph, beyond the rope-holding, stooping figure identified as Chief Boatswain's Mate Harvey Wahab. A second mound is also visible beyond the head of the grave. Two shovels are visible, one to the left of the legs of an unidentified man, and the other behind the man's left hand. The original photograph did not disclose where the second mound of earth had come from, but the enlargement did. Directly to the left rear of the man with the tattoo on his right forearm—Chief Boatswain's Mate Arnold Tolson—there is clear evidence of an open grave. Also, beyond the head of the grave, visible between Tolson's left arm and his body, is still another mound of excavated earth. The foot of the second grave can be seen between the right arm and legs of the unidentified Coast Guardsman in the left foreground.

The enlarged photograph dispelled the lingering question in the author's mind as to whether the graves were correctly marked. The photograph confirms that they are labeled properly.

But the obvious question that still remains unanswered is this: why were the two graves dug diagonally rather than parallel? And why were the two unknown seamen interred in a reversed diagonal? It is possible that, in the simultaneous digging of two graves, the men chose spots from which they would not be tossing excavated earth into each other's way.

The cemetery as it appeared in July 1969 after refurbishing by the crew of H.M.S. *Eagle*

CHAPTER VI

The Cemetery Today

TODAY THE LITTLE CEMETERY receives sporadic but loving care. Periodically some local citizen, boy scout group, or patriotic or civic organization cleans the area and places flowers and wreaths on the graves. Yet actual authority seems to be exercised by no one. In reply to a letter by the author to the Commonwealth War Graves Commission in London asking about the question of responsibility, the Commission replied ambiguously that "the Commission are only responsible for the four Commonwealth war graves on Ocracoke Island (Cunningham) Cemetery." However, the Commission seems to have appointed no agent to care for and maintain the site, nor are any funds dispersed locally for the purpose. Despite this apparent lack of official care, the little cemetery fares well—thanks to the sympathy, interest, and respect of the local citizens.

Not long ago the cemetery underwent a semiofficial British refurbishing, courtesy of the Royal Navy. On the afternoon of 2 July 1969, when the author was visiting the site with Miss Fulcher, a party of British naval personnel made an unexpected visit to Ocracoke. Five seamen, led by Chief Petty Officer D. R. E. Rowles, arrived in a station wagon driven by a U.S. seaman. The back of the wagon was filled with lumber—"English timber," they noted—

straight off the aircraft carrier H.M.S. *Eagle*, then making a brief stop at Norfolk. The *Eagle*'s skipper had learned of the graves and had asked for volunteers from his crew to tidy up the site. With enthusiasm the work party broke out saws, shovels, hammers, and nails. In minutes they had begun removing worn posts, rails, and pickets, and were replacing these with their good "English timbers." A Royal Navy photographer took still photos and motion pictures, proof that the British and their English-speaking cousins in America still remember and care to honor in a small way men who died in freedom's cause; and that this little spot that is forever England will not be neglected by its countrymen.

The entire story of the *Bedfordshire* and her crewmen is filled with coincidences, like the chance meeting of Brown and Cunningham, the oddity of the six flags, of Wahab Howard and Cunningham's watch, of Jack Willis and the razor, and a more recent one involving Mrs. Robert T. Probst of Louisville, Kentucky. In June 1963 Dr. and Mrs. Probst were vacationing in Ocracoke. While eating lunch in one of the restaurants, they purchased a little booklet about the island. When Mrs. Probst came to the reference to the British cemetery, she and her husband decided to pay a visit to the spot.

As Mrs. Probst gazed over the white fencing at the four stone crosses, she read the names of Cunningham and Craig. The names meant nothing to her at the time. It was not until later, when she told her mother, Mrs. Rycroft, of seeing the graves, that Stanley Craig's visit was recalled and the fact that it had been Craig who had left his dog tags on the Rycrofts' bathroom door.

Mrs. Probst had been a girl of eighteen when the *Bedfordshire* visited the Brooklyn Navy Yard, and like her mother she too had made lifelong friendships with relatives of the crew. One such friendship was with Mrs. Olive White, whose husband Charles was a radio operator aboard the *Bedfordshire* with young Stanley Craig. He also had been a guest in the Rycroft home. In fact, Mrs. White told her that Craig had been a very close friend of her husband and a visitor in their home. Mrs. White was left a widow with two very young children, a boy Lester and a girl Glenys.

Not too long ago Mrs. White fulfilled a wish and came to the United States to see Mrs. Rycroft and Mrs. Probst, who had been such good friends to her husband and who had had such a warm correspondence with her over the years. Mrs. Probst had planned to take Mrs. White to Ocracoke, but the trip did not work out, perhaps fortunately, since Mrs. Probst felt that Mrs. White was distinctly relieved when the trip was canceled.

Undoubtedly there are other such warm friendships that evolved from the little ship's short stay in American waters. Perhaps these friendships are a small but partially offsetting compensation to the crewmen's families for the loss of their kin in a common cause.

Ocracoke Village, nestled around Silver Lake, still retains the intriguing charm born of a bygone era, though the motel, restaurant, and gift shop signs remind one that

Ocracoke has become a favorite tourist attraction. Paved roads and a free forty-five-minute ferry ride across Hatteras Inlet make the trip to Ocracoke from nearby Hatteras, Nags Head, Kitty Hawk, and Kill Devil Hills a most pleasant one. With luck one can even glimpse the small wild pony herd on Ocracoke Island, now cared for by the National Park Service. Park service historians, incidentally, doubt the legends that attribute the ancestry of the ponies to shipwrecked Arabian horses.

The picturesque little cemetery, shaded in a grove of low trees and shrubs, is being visited more and more as the flow of summer tourists rises every year. And one's memory of it is made fast by the appropriate home-made bronze plaque on the cemetery fence, which is inscribed with Rupert Brooke's unforgettable lines (albeit the engraver erred in his quote):

> If I should die think only this of me:
> That that [sic] there's some corner
> Of a foreign field that is forever England.

APPENDIX A

The Fate of the *U-558*

OFFICIAL GERMAN RECORDS state that the *U-558* was sunk off Cape Ortegal in the Bay of Biscay on 20 July 1943 by Allied aircraft and that there were no survivors. A search of U.S. Navy and U.S. Army Air Force files confirmed the presumed kill of a U-boat on that date and location by two antisubmarine aircraft, a U.S. Liberator from the 19th Squadron, 479th Group, piloted by First Lieutenant C. F. Gallmier, and an RAF Halifax of the 58th Squadron.

Lieutenant Gallmier's debriefing report told of spotting two large 740-ton U-boats on the surface a little after noon of 20 July at 45°10′ north latitude and 09°43′ west longitude. Gallmier attacked and promptly ran into heavy antiaircraft fire, as Admiral Doenitz had doubled the armament on his subs in a vain attempt to give them a chance of surviving against aircraft. The fire from the U-boats was so intense that Gallmier swerved into a rain squall and in doing so lost sight of the two boats. Swinging out of the squall, he spotted what he described as a 570-ton sub, probably a VII C boat, whereas the others were probably larger Type IX boats. Gallmier began an attack run from the port quarter. More antiaircraft fire was directed at the American plane, and the Liberator received hits in the port fuselage and the port inboard engine. Gallmier's attempt to feather the prop was unsuccessful, and he therefore decided he had to break off the fight. But as Gallmier cleared the area, he saw an RAF Halifax come in on a strafing run and drop a stick of bombs or depth charges that completely straddled the U-boat. He felt that the Britisher had finished her off. But he also reported that prisoners were later recovered.

Confirmation of this account exists in the U.S. Navy records as well, in what were called Assessment Reports—formal evaluations of reported sub sinkings. According to Assessment Report 3816A of the 19th Squadron, USAAF, and Report 3816B of the 58th Squadron, RAF, copies of which are held in the U.S. Navy Archives, the attack was given a rating of A, signifying a certain or sure sinking. According to account 3816A, the pilot of the B-24 Liberator (Gallmier) spotted a 570-ton U-boat on the surface a little after noon on 20 July 1943. He described her as being of the double bandstand type, meaning she had been modified by the addition of an extended platform aft of the conning tower to hold additional antiaircraft guns. In his report Gallmier described the sub as gray-colored. He reported making a strafing run, seeing a depth charge exploding close to the sub, receiving flak damage that precluded his making a second attack, and seeing an RAF Halifax also make an attack. As he left the area, the sub was going down, and there were thirty to forty bodies in the water.

According to U.S. Navy historians, the British companion report described the sub as a 740-ton boat with gray and brown camouflage. The Halifax aircraft also claimed the sub as sunk and took photographs of some of the U-boat's crew in the water, some alive and in a dingy. The Halifax made another pass over the listing sub and dropped five depth charges that straddled her, three on one side and two on the other. Another pass over the vanished sub's bubbling spot showed three men in a dingy, with more men trying to get in.

In view of the mention by both pilots of seeing and, in the case of the RAF pilot, of photographing survivors of the sub on a raft, it seemed quite possible that some of the crew could have survived, either by drifting to the Spanish or Portuguese coast, 100 miles away at the nearest point, or by being recovered by British surface vessels or aircraft. Several attempts to verify such a possibility from British and German sources proved fruitless, but the author remained stubbornly unconvinced.

Then came the interesting piece of information in a recent book, *Iron Coffins*, by Herbert Werner, a former U-boat commander and now a U.S. citizen. Werner tells of his boat's intercepting the following radio message on 20 July 1943 from the *U-558*, "Aircraft Attacked Sinking Imprisonment *U-558*." The key word that caught the author's eye was "imprisonment." Unless such an event was imminent, why was it included in the message? Werner was asked to elaborate, but he could add little other than to say that he had known Krech briefly at Brest and that he too had heard there had been survivors.

The evidence seemed too strong to support the "no survivors" theme of the official records. After all, a sub lost at sea would be stricken from the rolls, and any repatriation of personnel some three years later would never catch up with the earlier war diary records of the U-boat high command. A check with British authorities of POW interrogations turned up nothing, so the author turned in June 1971 to a German U-boat historian, Jurgen Rohwer, of Stuttgart. The evidence was given to him and a request made that, perhaps through other ex-U-boat men or a veteran's group, he try to learn if anyone had survived the *U-558*.

To the author's delight Rohwer responded a month later to say he had learned that Gunther Krech, another officer, and three men had been taken prisoner of war by the British and that Krech was now living in Wuppertal, Germany. Unfortunately, repeated attempts to contact Krech have failed.

The *U-558* was sunk at a time when the tide of war had not only turned but had become almost one-sided in favor of the Allies. The development of airborne radar and the advent of the small aircraft carrier doomed the U-boat, and beginning in July 1943, the Allies were slaughtering German subs at a rate that virtually destroyed Doenitz's fleet. Thirty-three U-boats were killed that month by radar-carrying antisubmarine aircraft. Seven went down in the Bay of Biscay in the first twenty days, and ten of the next seventeen that put out from the channel ports were lost. The Germans tried in every way they could imagine to counter the attack, to no avail. Their counter-radar efforts failed; they increased their antiaircraft armament and tried, unsuccessfully, running in groups to neutralize the swarming planes; to submerge made them slow-moving easy targets for the avalanche of depth charges that inevitably followed. In view of the hideous loss rate the U-boats were suffering, it is remarkable that their morale remained as high as it did, even though, as Werner points out in *Iron Coffins*, when they put to sea in 1943, they knew their chances of returning were very slim.

But Gunther Krech was apparently a thorough skipper and had done all that was in his power to assure his crew a chance of survival, for the official World War II British history of the war at sea gives Kapitanleutnant Krech specific mention and praise regarding the sinking of the *U-558*.

... [Her skipper] had taken great trouble to train his crew in anti-aircraft defence, and during the first part of his homeward passage from a patrol off Portugal he reaped his reward by not only surviving several attacks, but also damaging the attackers. On the 20th of July, however, when he was almost through the zone covered by our air patrols, he was attacked by a U.S. Army Liberator and damaged it; but his boat was severely injured by another aircraft of the same squadron. Then an R.A.F. Halifax arrived, joined in the fight and finished off the enemy. The fight had been a gallant one.*

* *The War at Sea: 1939–45*, a United Kingdom Military History (London: Roskill, n.d.), III, Pt. 1, 25.

Recovery and Burial
of Other *Bedfordshire* Crewmen

T HE BODY OF A THIRD identifiable crew member of
H.M.S. *Bedfordshire* washed ashore near Swanquar-
ter, North Carolina, sometime in late May or June 1942.
Although the body was in a highly decomposed condition, a
Royal Navy identification tag identified it as that of Seaman
Alfred Dryden. Lieutenant Forrest Dunstan, now an attor-
ney in Elizabeth City, North Carolina, was a district intelligence officer, and the finding of the body was reported to
him. Association of Seaman Dryden with the *Bedfordshire*
was made later by Aycock Brown, who had, by that time,
obtained the trawler's crew listing.

Seaman Dryden was first interred in a public cemetery
near the Hyde County Poor House, and a fee was paid
to a local undertaker for services and the emplacement
of a marker. The installation of a marker was never ac-
complished, however, because the burial occurred before
identification was actually confirmed. The presence of an
identification tag on the remains meant little to the American authorities without official reports stating that there
was such a person in the Royal Navy and that he was missing in action.

After determining that Dryden was definitely one of the
Bedfordshire's crew, Brown endeavored to have the re-

mains transferred to the Ocracoke cemetery, but for undisclosed reasons, the body was reinterred instead in the Oak Grove Baptist Cemetery at Creeds, Virginia, on 2 February 1943. At that time, a full military funeral was held, with both U.S. Navy and Royal Navy personnel in attendance. Dryden's grave is marked now and is grave number three in lot fifty-seven, registered in the name of the British Admiralty.

The grave of another man possibly from the *Bedfordshire* is located near the Coast Guard Station at Cape Hatteras. This body was recovered on 21 May 1942, and according to Brown, who attempted unsuccessfully to identify it, the remains were virtually skeletal. But the timing of the recovery gives a degree of credibility to the theory that the man was from the *Bedfordshire*.

Regrettably, the grave, at the time of this writing, is in a disreputable state, showing evidence of desecration and total neglect. It is on a two-grave site about 100 yards north of the Coast Guard headquarters, about 160 feet down a little sandy lane called Old Pond Road, and 60 feet to the right. The site is completely covered over in a veritable tangle of vines, brush, and shrubbery. Only through the sharp memory of Dudley Burrus of Hatteras was the site located. Burrus, a former Coast Guard chief stationed at Hatteras, took great personal pride in maintaining the graves during his tenure of office. It had previously been the proud task of Chief Columbus Miller, who in 1944 had made concrete headstones for the two graves and had enclosed the site with a fence.

Today there is no vestige of the fencing, the stones have been broken and overturned, and one would have to be extremely lucky to find the spot without knowing its location fairly well. The Coast Guard says that the graves definitely are not on its land but on former North Carolina land deeded to the National Park Service. The author has requested that the National Park Service assume maintenance responsibility for the two graves—those of Britisher Michael Cairns, fourth engineer of the tanker *San Delfino*, whose body was recovered, identified, and buried on 9 May 1942, and of the unknown seaman on Cairns's right.

APPENDIX C

SERIAL NO. 189

OFFICIAL ADMIRALTY COMMUNIQUE

The Board of Admiralty regrets to announce the following casualties sustained in H.M.S. BEDFORDSHIRE, the loss of which has already been announced. Next-of-Kin have been notified.

OFFICERS
MISSING PRESUMED KILLED
Lieutenant R. B. DAVIS, R.N.R. (in command).
Temporary Sub-Lieutenant N. CLUTTERBUCK, R.N.V.R.
Temporary Sub-Lieutenant B. HALL, R.N.V.R.
KILLED
Temporary Sub-Lieutenant T. CUNNINGHAM, R.N.V.R.

R.N. RATINGS
MISSING PRESUMED KILLED

BARNES, Frederick W.	Engineman	LT/KX110465
BENNETT, Stanley	Ord. Seaman	LT/JX280397
BICKFORD, Leonard P.	Seaman	LT/JX206382
BOWEN, Ernest G.	Seaman	LT/JX140813
CARRUTHERS, Edward S.	Ord. Seaman	LT/JX286018
CERRINO, George W.	Ldg. Seaman R.N.R.	LT/X19054A
CLEMENCE, William F.	Ord. Seaman	LT/JX279627
CRAGG, Francis	Ord. Seaman	LT/JX265126
*CRAIG, Stanley R.	Ord. Telegraphist	D/JX228834

* "Missing Presumed Killed" was the category into which a lost serviceman was placed prior to the recovery and identification of a body. The fact that Seaman Craig is listed in this category indicates that fingerprint confirmation of the identification had not caught up with, and probably was considerably after, the casualty announcement.

DICK, John R.	Seaman	LT/JX224890
DICKS, Thomas H.	Ord. Seaman	LT/JX201998
DRYDEN, Alfred	Seaman	LT/JX241795
DUNCAN, Andrew W.	Chief Engineman R.N.R.	LT/X412 ET
FEATHERSTONE, Geoffrey	Ord. Telegraphist	D/JX197822
FISHER, George H.	Stoker 2nd class	LT/KX131433
FORD, Herbert	Seaman	LT/JX185319
KELLY, Joseph	Seaman	LT/JX253777
LEE, William	Ldg. Seaman R.N.R.	LT/X18212A
LUKINS, Ernest W.	A/Stoker Petty Officer	D/K65875
MC CRINDLE, Alex A.	Seaman	LT/JX198997
McKENZIE, Angus	Stoker	LT/KX114362
MALTBY, Frederick F.	Ldg. Seaman R.N.R.	LT/X19197A
MORTON, Ernest N.	Ord. Seaman	LT/JX303090
MYERS, William J.	Stoker	LT/KX132399
SMITTEN, Sidney W.	Ord. Seaman	LT/JX281103
STONE, Percy E.	Seaman	LT/JX185337
SWEENEY, John	Ord. Seaman	LT/JX299567
TRAVELL, Charles T.	Ord. Signalman	D/JX233510
WATSON, Thomas A.	Ord. Signalman	D/JX172255
WHITE, Charles W.	Ord. Telegraphist	C/JX258523
WILLIAMS, Leslie J.	Stoker 2nd class	LT/KX130958

R.C.N. RATINGS
MISSING PRESUMED KILLED

DAVIS, Russell	Ord. Seaman R.C.N.	V.26270
MC CAULEY, James L.	Ord. Seaman R.C.N.	V.16559

APPENDIX D

SPECIAL ORDER

DEDICATION OF CUNNINGHAM CEMETERY
CEREMONIES AND SCHEDULE OF EVENTS
1330, Sunday, December 27, 1942

UNIFORM OF THE DAY:
Officers: Service Blues, white hat cover,
with side arms.
Enlisted Men: Dress Blues, white hat.
Firing Squad: Dress Blues, white hat, with
leggings and webbed belts.

ASSEMBLE AT FRONT, CAPTAIN PAUL JONES BARRACKS.
Order of Formation will be:
A. Bugler.
B. Clergy.
C. Commanding Officer.
D. Officers.
E. Firing Squad, Ensign Meyer.
F. Enlisted Personnel.
(1) Chief Petty Officers.
(2) Naval Personnel.
(3) Coast Guard Personnel.
All officers and enlisted men of both Navy and Coast
Guard are invited to attend, but must fall in, in formation, pursuant to schedule, in the prescribed uniform.

AGENDA:
1. 1330–Parade to form in front of
Captain Paul Jones Barracks.
2. 1340–Parade to proceed to
Cunningham Cemetery.

79

(a) Officers form on left hand side
of cemetery facing inward.

(b) Firing squad form on right hand
side facing graves.

(c) Support Battalion will form abaft
firing squad.

3. Protestant Service by Reverend Wm. R. Dixon.
4. Catholic Service by Chaplain Donald J. Strange.
5. Taps.
6. The Salute.
7. Retreat.
8. At Captain Paul Jones Barracks–Dismissed.

(Signed)

Thos. W. Sheridan
Commander, D-V(G), USNR
Commanding Officer.

The Author

Born in Garden City, New York, but now a long-time resident of Manassas, Virginia, Van Naisawald acquired from his father early in life an interest in history and athletics and a fondness for the military services. He has been quite successful in blending these interests in a satisfying career that included twenty-five years as an active and reserve army officer and as a historian and professional writer. He is now employed in the latter capacity by the Department of the Army, in the Office of the Chief of Research and Development.

Mr. Naisawald did his undergraduate work at Virginia Military Institute and received a master's degree in history from the University of North Carolina. His writing career began in 1950, while he was serving with the Army's Office of the Chief of Military History. The Oxford University Press published his book, *Grape and Canister*, which received unusually fine reviews and carried an endorsement by the noted historian Bruce Catton. Mr. Naisawald has written more than a hundred historical and travel articles, which have appeared in various popular magazines and scholarly journals.